Koalas and Kangaroos

Strange Animals of Australia

by Toni Eugene

BOOKS FOR YOUNG EXPLORERS
NATIONAL GEOGRAPHIC SOCIETY

This big red kangaroo can travel 25 feet in one hop.

Gray kangaroos jump across a wide, grassy field in Australia. Australia is a faraway land with water all around it. Kangaroos and many other kinds of animals that live there do not live anywhere else.

GRAY KANGAROOS *(kang-guh-ROOZ)*

They are different from other animals you may have seen.
Gray kangaroos move quickly on their strong back legs. They have
long, heavy tails that help them keep their balance as they hop.

3

Kangaroos are animals called marsupials. Most female marsupials have pouches like pockets.

4

Kangaroos live only in Australia. They are the biggest marsupials.
A baby kangaroo, or joey, puts its head into its mother's pouch
to drink her milk. When the joey is frightened, it leaps into her pouch.
Safe and cozy, the joey pokes out its head to nibble grass.

GRAY KANGAROOS ARE MARSUPIALS *(mar-SOO-pea-ulz)*.

RED-NECKED WALLABIES *(WOLL-uh-beez)*

Two smaller kangaroos called wallabies sniff each other.
They push each other with their short front legs,
and they kick at each other with their long back legs.
There are many kinds of these small kangaroos.
Some, called rock wallabies, live in rocky places.

As it moves about, a possum wraps its toes and tail around a branch. Possums are marsupials that spend most of their time in trees. They use their hind feet like hands. Babies ride on their mother's back. They cling tightly to her fur.

A sugar glider licks sweet nectar from a flower. Whoosh! This marsupial glides by stretching out flaps of skin on its body.

SUGAR GLIDER

A fuzzy koala sits high in a tree.
Its sharp claws help it hold on.
Koalas are among the best-known
of all the animals of Australia.
A koala nibbles eucalyptus leaves,
almost the only food it eats.
Its button nose and furry ears
make it look like a teddy bear,
but it is not a bear at all.
Koalas are marsupials.
When a baby grows too big
for its mother's pouch, it rides
on her back instead.

KOALA *(kuh-WAH-luh)*
IN A EUCALYPTUS *(yoo-kuh-LIP-tus)* TREE

The numbat lives in forests.
It uses its long nose
to find termites and ants
in logs and in the ground.

NUMBAT

WOMBAT

The wombat eats grass
and roots. It lives alone.
Wombats dig large holes
where they often sleep
during the day.
Wombats and numbats
are also marsupials.
What strange names
Australian animals have!

The rabbit-eared bandicoot has long ears like a rabbit's. It is as small as a rabbit, too. The bandicoot uses its pointed nose and sharp claws to get insects to eat. This marsupial digs deep, winding tunnels where it lives and hides.

RABBIT-EARED BANDICOOT *(BAN-dih-koot)*

Standing on its thin hind legs,
a dunnart sniffs, looks, and listens.
The dunnart has a tiny pouch. It is
one of the smallest marsupials—
as small as a mouse. It is
also called a marsupial mouse.
A native cat chews a piece of meat.
This animal is about the size
of a house cat, and it hunts
at night. The native cat is
a marsupial and not a cat at all.
Tasmanian devils fight over food.
Their sharp, pointed teeth make
these marsupials look very fierce.
They really are shy animals,
only about the size of small dogs.

NATIVE CAT

TASMANIAN DEVILS (taz-MAY-nee-un DEV-ulz)

On webbed feet, a platypus waddles slowly toward the water.
This animal has a flat tail like a beaver's and a bill like a duck's.
It looks very odd! Long ago, when scientists first saw a platypus,
they thought someone had put parts of different animals together.
A platypus is covered with thick fur, and it lays eggs.
Its tail and feet help it swim. It uses its bill to find food underwater.

PLATYPUS *(PLAT-ih-pus)*

This animal is called
an echidna. It is
covered with spines
like a porcupine's.
It shoots out
its long, sticky tongue
to catch ants.

ECHIDNA *(ih-KID-nuh)*

An echidna is also called a spiny anteater.
Like a platypus, an echidna lays eggs.
When an echidna is frightened,
it may burrow into the ground to hide.
It quickly digs a hole with its strong claws.
Soon only its back shows above ground.

An echidna has another way of protecting its soft body.
It curls into a ball. Its sharp spines stick out so that it looks
like a big pincushion. This echidna is on its back. Do you see its feet?

Australia has many kinds of birds. Emus stand as tall as grown-ups. These birds cannot fly, but they can run fast. A cassowary is big, too, and it also cannot fly. When it runs in the forest, it may push branches aside with the hard top of its head. Frogmouths were named for their wide bills. A kookaburra makes a sound like a person laughing.

CASSOWARY *(KASS-uh-werry)*

EMUS *(EE-myooz)*

TAWNY FROGMOUTHS

KOOKABURRA (COOK-uh-bur-uh)

Three baby black swans rest
on a pile of sticks in a lake.
Their mother climbs up out
of the water to be with them.
Australian swans are black,
not white like the ones we know.
Soon these baby swans will begin
to lose their fluffy gray down.

They will grow black feathers
and look like their parents.
Black swans are graceful birds.
One paddles quietly on the lake.

SATIN BOWERBIRDS

A satin bowerbird is building a kind of playhouse called a bower.
He does this to attract a mate. He has collected blue clothespins
to decorate his bower. Blue is the bowerbird's favorite color.
After the bowerbird finishes building, he dances for a green female.
When a male lyrebird has attracted a mate, he swings his tail feathers
over his head and spreads them out. They look like a silver fan.

LYREBIRD

GALAHS *(guh-LAHZ)*

Gray-and-pink parrots called galahs sail through the air. Rosy feathers on their heads make them look as if they are wearing masks.
A rainbow lorikeet perches in a mulberry bush to eat the juicy berries. Its bright feathers are the colors of a rainbow. A honeyeater balances on top of a flowering plant to pick out insects with its long bill.

RAINBOW LORIKEET (LAW-rih-keet)

HONEYEATER

Hiss! A frilled lizard opens its mouth wide and raises the skin
around its neck. It does this to scare away enemies.
A thorny devil is protected by pointed scales like sharp thorns.
Because it is frightened, a bearded dragon puffs out the scaly skin
below its mouth. Australia's biggest lizards are goannas like this one.
When they stand on their hind legs, some goannas may be as tall as you.

THORNY DEVIL

BEARDED DRAGON

GOANNA (go-ANN-uh)

FRILLED LIZARD

29

At sunset, a red kangaroo stops on a low hill and looks back.
Where do you think it is going? What other animals will it see?
Many of these animals will be different from the ones we know best.

And many of them live only in Australia. Some have pouches. Some stay in trees. Some are beautiful. And some are very strange. Which Australian animals would you like to meet?

Published by The National Geographic Society
Gilbert M. Grosvenor, *President;* Melvin M. Payne, *Chairman of the Board;*
Owen R. Anderson, *Executive Vice President;* Robert L. Breeden, *Vice President,
Publications and Educational Media*

Prepared by The Special Publications Division
Donald J. Crump, *Director*
Philip B. Silcott, *Associate Director*
William L. Allen, William R. Gray, *Assistant Directors*

Staff for this Book
Margery G. Dunn, *Managing Editor*
Geraldine Linder, *Picture Editor*
Marianne R. Koszorus, *Art Director*
Gail N. Hawkins, *Researcher*
Carol A. Rocheleau, *Illustrations Secretary*

Engraving, Printing, and Product Manufacture
Robert W. Messer, *Manager*
George V. White, *Production Manager*
David V. Showers, *Production Project Manager*
Mark R. Dunlevy, Richard A. McClure, Raja D. Murshed, Christine A. Roberts, Gregory Storer, *Assistant Production Managers*
Mary A. Bennett, Katherine H. Donohue, *Production Staff Assistants*

Debra A. Antonini, Nancy F. Berry, Pamela A. Black, Nettie Burke, Jane H. Buxton, Claire M. Doig, Rosamund Garner, Victoria D. Garrett,
   Virginia A. McCoy, Cleo Petroff, Victoria I. Piscopo, Tammy Presley, Katheryn M. Slocum, Jenny Takacs, *Staff Assistants*

Consultants
Dr. Glenn O. Blough, Karen O. Strimple, *Educational Consultants*
Lynda Ehrlich, *Reading Consultant*
Guy A. Greenwell, Senior Ornithologist, Department of Conservation, National Zoological Park; Robin Hill; Frances Irish, Division of Reptiles and
   Amphibians, Smithsonian Institution; Dr. Robert J. Whelan, Research Fellow, Department of Zoology, University of Florida, *Scientific Consultants*

Illustrations Credits
© George Leavens, 1979 (1); Jen and Des Bartlett (2-3, 4 upper, 7 upper, 7 lower left and right, 10 left, 30-31); Kojo Tanaka, ANIMALS ANIMALS
(4 lower); Tom McHugh, National Audubon Society Collection, Photo Researchers (4-5, 32); Douglass Baglin, NHPA (6-7); Stanley Breeden
(8 upper left, 8-9); Ralph and Daphne Keller (8 upper right); M. K. and I. M. Morcombe (9, 14, 15 upper, 27 lower right); J. Baylor Roberts
(10 right); © Robert L. Dunne, BRUCE COLEMAN INC. (11); Garry Lewis, Photographic Library of Australia (12, 15 lower, 21 left); Hans and Judy
Beste, ANIMALS ANIMALS (12-13 upper, 29 right); A. G. (Bert) Wells, Oxford Scientific Films (12-13 lower); Robin Smith, Photographic Library
of Australia (16-17, 29 upper); Douglass Baglin, PHL Globe Photos (17 upper); Australian Information Service (18 upper); PITCH, Jean-Paul Ferrero
(18 lower); David C. Rentz, BRUCE COLEMAN INC. (18-19); National Geographic Photographer Bates Littlehales (20, 21 upper right); Harold T.
Coss (20-21); Angabe A. Schmidecker, ALPHA (22); Dianne Dietrich-Leis, ALPHA (22-23); Philip Green (24, 25 upper); L. H. Smith (25 lower left
and right); Jim Frazier, Mantis Wildlife Films (26-27); Len Robinson, Frank Lane (27 lower left); Warren Garst, TOM STACK & ASSOCIATES (28);
M. K. Morcombe, NHPA (29 center left); cover photograph: A. Foley, Leo de Wys Inc.

Library of Congress CIP Data
Eugene, Toni.
   Koalas and kangaroos.

   (Books for young explorers)
   Supt. of Docs. no.: LC 1.2:K79
   Summary: Describes the characteristics and behavior of different kinds of Australian mammals, birds, and reptiles.
   1. Zoology—Australia—Juvenile literature.   [1. Zoology—Australia. 2. Australia]   I. National Geographic Society (U. S.)   II. Title.   III. Series.
   QL338.E93   599.0994   81-607859
   ISBN 0-87044-403-4 (regular binding)   AACR2
   ISBN 0-87044-408-5 (library binding)

QUOKKA *(KWAH-kuh)*

A little wallaby
called a quokka
munches on a leaf.

Cover: A baby koala
clings to its mother.